MEDICAL MALPRACTICE *And* WRONGFUL DEATH *In New York*

Answers To Tough Questions That Can Arise In Your Case

DAVID M. ODDO, ESQ.

Jacobs & Whitehall
73-03 Bell Blvd, #10
Oakland Gardens, NY 11364
(888) 570-7338
www.jacobsandwhitehall.com

Ordering Information:

Quantity sales. Special discounts are available on quantity purchases by corporations, associations, and others. For details, contact the publisher at the address above.

Orders by U.S. trade bookstores and wholesalers. Please contact Jacobs & Whitehall: Tel: (888) 991-2766 or visit www.jacobsandwhitehall.com.

Printed in the United States of America

Published in 2021

ISBN: 978-1-954506-18-3

PREFACE

David M. Oddo is a prominent New York City trial attorney who has represented clients in a number of high profile civil and criminal cases throughout New York State. He was named to New York's 2021 Metro Super Lawyers list, an honor reserved for those lawyers who exhibit excellence in practice with only 5% of attorneys in the New York Metro area receiving this distinction. According to TopVerdict.com, Mr. Oddo obtained the highest medical malpractice settlement in New York State in 2020 (15 million dollars for a client who sustained severe and permanent injuries as the result of a misdiagnosed stroke) and has been featured in *Top 100 Magazine* in 2020 and 2021, as well as being highlighted in *Top Lawyers Northeast* and *Top Lawyers New York*, by *Arrive Magazine* in 2011. He was named to *City and State* Magazine's 50 Over 50 list of distinguished and impactful New Yorkers (2018 and 2019). In 2018, *City and State* Magazine named Mr. Oddo to its Law Power

50 List, recognizing the most influential lawyers in New York State.

He also serves as a lecturer to the profession on topics concerning trial practice, medical malpractice, the economist's role in trial preparation and presentation, as well as the role and function of the U.S. Civil Justice System. Mr. Oddo is a former state prosecutor, serving in the Nassau County District Attorney's Office from 1989-1993. Mr. Oddo also enjoys the highest ranking of 10 from AVVO. He has been a contributing editor for *The Hill* and has published Op-eds on civil justice issues in various newspapers across the state.

Mr. Oddo is a *Past President,* of the New York State Trial Lawyers Association (NYSTLA) and is a *Fellow* of the American Bar Foundation, a distinction given to less than one percent of lawyers licensed to practice in each jurisdiction. He is a member of the American Bar Association, American Association of Justice, New York State Bar Association, Bronx County Bar Association and the New York County Lawyer's

Association, as well as a number of other local bar associations. He was admitted to the New York State and Connecticut State Bar in 1990, and he is also admitted to practice in the Federal Courts of the United States District Courts, for the Southern and Eastern Districts of New York (1993). In May 2016, Mr. Oddo was admitted to practice before the United States Supreme Court.

DEDICATION

This book is dedicated to my past and present clients who have lost loved ones to malpractice or have been victims of avoidable medical errors. Your individual stories of courage, faith and resilience have inspired and motivated me to be the best trial attorney I can be. Thank you for your trust and confidence in my firm and for the privilege of representing you.

Also, to the lawyers who have dedicated their professional lives to representing the injured, I salute your commitment, purpose and resolve in fighting for those unable to fight for themselves against powerful interests. As I mention in the book, this line of work is not for the faint of heart. It is for those who view their profession not just as a job, but as a calling.

– David M. Oddo

DISCLAIMER

This publication is intended to be used for educational purposes only. No legal advice is being given, and no attorney-client relationship is intended to be created by reading this material. The author assumes no liability for any errors or omissions or for how this book or its contents are used or interpreted, or for any consequences resulting directly or indirectly from the use of this book. For legal or any other advice, please consult an experienced attorney or the appropriate expert, who is aware of the specific facts of your case and is knowledgeable in the law in your jurisdiction.

Oddo & Babat, P.C.

8 West 38th Street
10th floor
New York, NY 10018
(646) 828 1980
www.oddobabat.com

TESTIMONIALS

"On behalf of my family, I would like to express our sincere thanks to you for representing our family following the tragic loss of my husband and a lovely dad. We especially appreciated all you did in working the legal details, keeping us informed, your responsiveness to questions throughout the process and negotiating the settlement. Thank you for your support to our family during this challenging time in our lives. I cannot describe how satisfied I am about the way Mr. Oddo and his team handled my case. First, the way they handle their clients is top notch; they always return phone calls and email messages, even on Saturdays! David Oddo is a very professional lawyer who is very honest and knowledgeable. What really impressed me is the way, at trial, he described to the jury my personality, in particular the details about way my family lived our life before and after my husband's death. It was like if he knew us for a lifetime. He is also very caring and a good listener and kept me positive during the most negative times of my life. I have to say I will always consider him a friend for all the support given to me. It also turned out in the end that the amount we recovered was much higher than what we expected, so I cannot really ask for more! Now I can see why there are so many positive testimonials about this law firm. I highly recommend this law firm. Thank you!"

– Madeline A

****

"I consulted with David the first time a couple of years ago on a serious matter that affected a very close member of my family. Not expecting a good experience from this serious situation coupled with an attorney consultation, the entire thing surprised me as it was pleasant, professional, and completely successful. We found him clear, direct, generous, and extremely knowledgeable throughout the process. I give my very strongest recommendation."

– Avvo Reviews

****

"Odds & Babat law firm has handled my family and friends' legal issues for over a decade. They are professional, knowledgeable and friendly, these are characteristics one wants when choosing a law firm. Thanks for always being there when they needed you."

– Luis V.

****

"I have been a client of this Law firm for over a decade. Utilizing their services numerous times throughout the years. I must say, the honesty, sincerity, and family atmosphere of this law firm is an almost obsolete characteristic in today's law practices. David Oddo, and Eric Babat are as professional and caring as they come. I feel extremely comfortable referring this practice to you as I do to my friends and family. Try them for all your legal needs. You will not be disappointed."

– Joey S.

****

"Excellent service and representation from this law firm especially Mr. Eric Babat whose guidance truth professionalism and hard work guided me to the successful outcome that I acquired regarding my case. What a way to end the year I will be eternally grateful for everyone who worked on my case and those who introduced me to this firm and their standard of excellence thank you Obina and Judge Jackson for your introduction to Eric Babat and that entire law firm."

– Janine

****

"David Oddo is amazing. After being referred to me 10 years ago, I have had the occasion to call on him to represent me on a serious personal injury issue... His mind is amazing, his manner is focused and generous and he was completely clear about my cases, what I could expect from the situation, and, most amazing, he always manages to put me completely at ease, even while I was in great pain from my injuries.
Wish I could give him 10 stars!"

–S. Leifer

****

Table Of Contents

INTRODUCTION

My name is David Oddo, and I am a partner and senior trial attorney at the law firm Oddo & Babat, P.C.

I began my legal career as a state prosecutor in the Nassau County District Attorney's Office, where I prosecuted a wide variety of criminal matters, on behalf of the victims of those crimes. As much as I enjoyed and valued public service, I entered private practice in 1993, in order to represent a different kind of victim: people who have been seriously injured as the result of the negligent, reckless or wilful conduct of others. I have dedicated my professional life toward the goal of obtaining justice for people through our civil justice system. I take great pride in fighting for those who do not have the ability or means to take on the insurance companies, big corporations, hospitals, nursing homes etc…especially after their lives have been turned upside down by catastrophic injury suffered through no fault of their own.

I have never aspired to represent banks or corporations; I have always been called to represent individuals and their families, and to try to make a real difference in people's lives. Since I entered private practice almost 30 years ago, I have focused on representing victims of medical malpractice and catastrophic personal injury.

My firm concentrates its practice in the areas of medical malpractice, automobile accidents, premises liability and other general negligence cases. We are also one of the leading firms representing survivors of childhood sexual abuse, whether the abuse was by an individual, organization or institution.

This book is designed to address many of the misconceptions and common questions surrounding medical malpractice and wrongful death in New York, which are areas of law that present unique and challenging issues. I believe that a better understanding of these issues will benefit both our clients and the attorneys who represent those injured through negligent acts. For that reason, this book is also meant to answer some of the tougher questions that arise in medical malpractice and wrongful death cases. Victims of medical malpractice and those who have lost loved ones through the negligence of others face daunting personal challenges. Having to navigate a lawsuit without a skilled, experienced trial attorney should not be one of them. For the attorney, please know that these cases are not for the faint of heart. It is well known that the successful trial attorney is not only armed with the necessary experience, knowledge and trial skills, but also with extraordinary courage, conviction and empathy.

SECTION 1: MEDICAL MALPRACTICE

CHAPTER 1

MEDICAL MALPRACTICE IN NEW YORK: THE BASICS

Medical malpractice is negligence on the part of a doctor or other health care provider. It occurs when there is 1) a doctor-patient relationship and 2) that doctor or health care provider deviates from an accepted or standard medical practice, and 3) injury or the death of a patient occurs as a result of that deviation. The standard is compared to what an average medical professional would have done when faced with the same circumstances. In order to prevail in a medical malpractice case, the patient must show that a competent doctor would have acted differently in the care and treatment of the patient. The doctor does not have to provide the "best" care, but rather has to provide care that is reasonable and in line with a customary standard of medical care. Simply not being satisfied with the results of your care is not enough to bring a claim.

General Negligence vs. Medical Malpractice

For those reasons, proving negligence in a medical malpractice case is a slightly different task than proving negligence in a general negligence case. For example, if someone sustains an injury after being rear-ended by another vehicle, all the injured party must show in order to obtain compensation is that; the other party failed to act reasonably in the operation and control of their vehicle; the lack of reasonableness caused the collision, and that their injuries are a direct result of that negligence.

In contrast, a person who has been injured as a result of medical malpractice must show that the health care provider deviated or departed from an accepted or standard medical practice. This may sound easier than it actually is, especially considering the fact that different health care providers receive different levels and degrees of medical training. However, it comes down to whether or not the standard of care was met. Was the care reasonable? Would a similarly situated physician have acted in the same way?

The second important difference between general negligence cases and medical malpractice cases has to do with filing requirements. To file a medical malpractice lawsuit under New York Civil Practice Law and Rules, Section 3012-a, the plaintiff must attach to the lawsuit a document called a Certificate of Merit. This certificate affirms that the attorney for the plaintiff has consulted with an expert physician, and that as a result of that consultation, the expert physician has opined that there is a reasonable ground for the commencement of a medical malpractice lawsuit, and that the claim is meritorious.

In other words, filing a medical malpractice lawsuit in New York requires a medical opinion from a licensed physician indicating that the case has merit. There is no such requirement when it comes to a general negligence case, such as one involving injuries sustained in an automobile collision.

The third—and perhaps most consequential—difference is that jurors tend to treat doctors differently from non-physician tortfeasors because of their special knowledge and experience. In doing so, jurors sometimes treat them differently than they do other negligent individuals because of the juror's own experience with doctors, whether it has been positive or negative. Furthermore, since most jurors do not have medical training and do not have experience in the medical field, it can be very challenging for some jurors to evaluate a defendant doctor's conduct.

Types of Medical Malpractice Cases

Medical malpractice can involve a wide array of medical scenarios. Examples include failure to diagnose a medical condition, delay in treating a medical condition, misdiagnosis of a heart attack, birth injuries such as a brachial plexus injury, Erbs palsy, cerebral palsy, or brain damage, gynecological malpractice, hospital negligence, emergency room errors, medication errors, anesthesia malpractice, and all types of surgical errors. Wrongful death can also fall under the umbrella of medical malpractice, as we will discuss in the chapters ahead.

The Plaintiff

Who can file a malpractice claim? A medical malpractice claim can, of course, be filed by the patient who was injured. However, what happens if the patient is now legally incapacitated, i.e., in a coma, or unable to understand the proceedings? In that case, a guardian of the person or of the property can be appointed by the court. With court approval, the guardian would assume the right to bring the claim on behalf of the injured and incapacitated party.

If the injured party is a minor (i.e., under the age of 18), then they cannot bring the lawsuit themselves; the parent or natural guardian of the minor would need to bring the lawsuit on the minor's behalf.

If the injured party is deceased, and their death was the direct result of the malpractice, then a wrongful death lawsuit can be brought by a personal representative of the decedent's estate.

The Defendant

A medical malpractice claim can be brought against an individual doctor or other healthcare provider (not limited to; a general practice physician, internist, OBGYN, radiologist, podiatrist, nurse, physician's assistant, dentist, hospital, nursing home, rehabilitation facility, etc…). Some lawsuits may include a number of parties such as a hospital, the treating physicians, physician assistants, nursing care facilities, and other medical facilities as defendants. Generally, a case can be brought against anyone who was negligent in providing medical care to the injured patient, and that negligence was the cause of the claimed injuries.

The Statute of Limitations

The statute of limitations for filing a medical malpractice claim in New York is two and a half years, and is governed by New York Civil Practice Law and

Rules section 214-a. The clock begins to run on the statute of limitations on the date that the medical negligence occurs. If the plaintiff fails to bring a lawsuit within those two and a half years, then they will be forever barred from bringing that claim. In other words, plaintiffs have one shot at filing a medical malpractice claim, and if they miss the two-and-a-half-year window of opportunity to bring a lawsuit, they are out of luck and will be forever barred from doing so. Anyone who suspects that they are the victim of malpractice should act quickly to schedule a consultation with an experienced medical malpractice lawyer.

- ***The Caveats***

There are some caveats to the above analysis. The first applies when there is continuous, ongoing treatment being provided by the offending physician, hospital, medical facility, etc.., after the negligence has occurred. Under these circumstances, the patient has two and a half years from the date of the last treatment for the condition in issue with that particular defendant. Be aware that courts have defined "continuous treatment" in a very specific way, so your attorney must be fully knowledgeable of those parameters. Simply continuing to visit your doctor regularly may not be enough to establish continuous treatment.

The second caveat has to do with what is called the discovery rule, which provides the patient with additional time to file a lawsuit, so long as the patient was unaware that a mistake or medical malpractice occurred at the time of the negligence, but discovers it later.

The discovery rule applies in only two situations. The first is when a physician leaves behind a foreign object (i.e., any object that was absolutely not meant to be implanted inside the patient's body like a sponge or surgical instrument) during a surgical procedure. If this occurs, the statute dictates that the patient has one year to file a claim, commencing from the date that they discovered the mistake or reasonably should have discovered the mistake.

The second situation in which the discovery rule applies is when a doctor (or other healthcare professional) negligently fails to diagnose a patient with cancer when they otherwise should have.

"Lavern's Law" (amending CPLR Sec. 214-(a) and Sec. 203(g)) was enacted in New York and signed into law on January 31, 2018, and changed the way the statute of limitations is calculated for these types of medical malpractice cases involving the failure to timely diagnose and treat cancer. Prior to the new law, if a patient discovered that their doctor missed a cancer diagnosis, they had 2½ years from the date of the missed diagnosis to commence a lawsuit. However, in many cases of delayed cancer diagnosis, the patient does not even realize that the diagnosis was missed until months or even years later, and by that time the statute of limitations has passed. Thanks to Lavern's Law, the statute of limitations now begins to run on the date the cancer is discovered, or when it should have reasonably been discovered by the patient. The plaintiff now has 2 ½ years to bring the action from that point, or 2 ½ years from the last date of treatment where there is continuous treatment for the same illness, injury or condition which gave rise to the cause of action (whichever is longer), provided that the action is started within 7 years of the malpractice (or last date of continuous treatment).

- *Suing a Municipality*

Please be aware that there is a much shorter period of time within which a patient must bring a claim if the defendant is a municipality, such as a county, city or state hospital, or an employee of the municipal facility. Keep in mind that some medical clinics, nursing homes and rehabilitation facilities can also be municipal entities. The attorney must be diligent to confirm whether or not the offending facility or personnel are actually municipal entities for purposes of the statute of limitations.

Generally, you have one year and ninety days to file a lawsuit against the City of New York. In order to file a lawsuit however, a Notice of Claim or its equivalent must be properly filed with the municipality within 90 days of the malpractice, though these time frames vary depending on the municipality being sued. Filing the Notice of Claim is a prerequisite to filing the lawsuit. Again, the statute of limitations varies depending on whether you are suing a city, state or local entity. Understanding the statute of limitations in medical malpractice cases is tricky and can be filled with legal landmines depending on the fact pattern of each individual case. It cannot be stressed enough that anyone who feels they have been a victim of malpractice should speak with an experienced attorney as soon as possible to determine the proper filing deadlines.

CHAPTER 2

PROVING A MEDICAL MALPRACTICE CASE

Generally, there are four elements to a viable medical malpractice case: (1) proof of a duty of care; (2) proof of a breach of that duty of care; (3) proof of causation; and (4) proof that the breach of duty of care caused damages.

Sometimes medical negligence, or a deviation from the standard of care, has occurred, but there are no resulting damages to the patient. There could also be a situation wherein a doctor or health care provider did not depart from a standard of care, but there were serious resulting medical complications. In other words, physical injuries may be a natural complication of a procedure, and not necessarily the fault of the doctor or health care provider.

Whether a medical malpractice case is viable comes down to whether or not it can be shown that a doctor or health care provider deviated from a level of care that a reasonable doctor or health care provider would have delivered under the same set of circumstances. It is equally critical for the plaintiff to prove that the deviation by the defendant caused the damages for which they are seeking compensation.

Attorney as Detective: Building a Strong Case

In building a strong medical malpractice case, there are at least four essential roles of the attorney.

1. Completing the Medical Record Puzzle

It is critical for the attorney to obtain the client's complete medical record as soon as possible. This requires obtaining from the client medical record authorizations under the Health Insurance Portability and Accountability Act of 1996 (HIPAA) in order to retrieve all of the pertinent medical records. This means a good portion of the client's entire medical history—not just the portion related to the medical negligence issue at hand. This includes obtaining all prior treatment records, diagnostic films and reports (e.g., X-rays, MRI scans, CT scans, mammograms, consultations, physical exams, lab results, etc.).

This is important because the attorney must identify whether the client had any known pre-existing medical conditions that could have been the cause of, or contributed to, the client's medical issues. The attorney must rule out the possibility that the injury was caused by something that occurred in the client's past medical history, unrelated to medical malpractice.

The attorney must prepare a timeline of both medical and non-medical events. This is done during a thorough interview with the client and other witnesses, as well as a careful evaluation of the medical records. The attorney should constantly add to the timeline as more medical information becomes available. I use an application called TimeLine Presenter by TimeLine Systems AS that integrates the client's medical records into a state-of-the-art timeline with graphics that can later be used at trial. Clients should be diligent in updating their lawyer on their current medical treatment and tests. The lawyer should regularly check in with the client and the client's health care providers to make sure the lawyer has all updated medical information.

Next, the attorney must secure a medical expert, or experts, in the relevant and associated medical field(s) to review the record in its entirety, and render an opinion with respect to whether or not the doctor, hospital, medical facility, nurse, or any other health care provider violated the standard of care. There are services like The Expert Institute that can recommend excellent, qualified and trustworthy physician experts to review the medical records in your case and determine whether your case has merit.

2. The Interviewing Process

To obtain as much information about the case and to identify potential witnesses, the attorney must interview the client, their family members, and anyone else who was present at the time of the alleged negligence, who could serve as a witness to the liability (i.e., the medical negligence) on the part of health care providers.

Interviewing family members, friends, and co-workers is also valuable to identify each element of damages suffered by the client. For instance, the client's family and friends might be able to make a statement about their observations of how the injuries affect your client's ability to perform their daily activities, changes in their behavior or persona, any physical limitations or restrictions, as well as any pain and suffering that they may have witnessed the client endure.

3. A Thorough Investigation

One of the most important steps for the attorney in investigating a medical malpractice claim is determining whether the potential defendants are municipal or private entities, as this will dictate the statute of limitations that applies to the case.

This requires a thorough investigation into all potential responsible parties. For instance, did the radiologist provide an inaccurate reading of the CT scan to the physician, who then relied on the erroneous reading thereby causing the negligent care? What about a case where a patient never received the proper medication after major surgery and suffered severe complications as a result? Did the physician negligently fail to order the medication? Or did the recovery room nurse fail to carry out the doctor's orders? Answering these types of questions requires a high level of investigative work and close attention to detail, but it is absolutely essential to building a successful case.

4. Dissecting the Damages

Another critical task for the attorney is to determine the nature and extent of the client's damages, as this will determine, in large part, the value of the case and what is a reasonable amount needed to fully compensate the client. To determine the full nature and extent of the client's damages, information must be gathered concerning lost wages and lost income, medical bills and expenses, and pain and suffering. In almost all cases, a calculation of the client's lost wages and future earnings will require the analysis of an economic expert.

Any and all harms and costs associated with the medical negligence must be identified and scrutinized in order to maximize adequate compensation for the client, including home care needs, home modifications, required medical devices, and physical therapy.

CHAPTER 3

VALUING A MEDICAL MALPRACTICE CASE

The value of a medical malpractice case will depend on a number of variables, such as the nature and extent of the injury, i.e., past and future pain and suffering, limitations and restrictions, the nature and extent of the provable economic damages, and projections regarding future medical needs.

Available Damages

A plaintiff who succeeds in proving their medical practice case is entitled to recover for both economic and non-economic damages. Generally, economic damages include past and future medical expenses and lost earnings, while non-economic damages include pain and suffering. If the injured patient is a minor, the parents can recover for loss of services, and the spouse of the injured party can also recover for Loss of consortium and/or loss of services.

No Cap on Non-Economic Damages

Unlike many other states, there is no cap on non-economic damages (i.e., the amount a jury can award for pain and suffering) in New York. Caps on non-economic damages do nothing more than prevent injured parties from being made whole and serve to protect tortfeasors from accountability. Thankfully, New York law recognizes the gross injustice of strict caps and instead places its trust in the civil jury system.

Case Study: An Undiagnosed Stroke

A former client of Oddo & Babat, suffered permanent disability when the emergency room staff failed to recognize and act upon signs of a stroke. If treated with a simple "clot buster" while in the emergency room, he would not have suffered any of his most seriously debilitating injuries. This extremely active 40-year-old man with a wife and two young children who had no prior physical problems, eventually found himself permanently confined to a wheelchair, unable to speak and move his legs, and impeded by cognitive difficulties as a result of the injuries he sustained from delay in diagnosis and treatment.

After proving that the defendants committed malpractice in failing to timely treat our client, and that delay caused his injuries, we had to assess the damages sustained by him and his family as a result. Under New York law, the client was entitled to be compensated for his past and future physical and emotional pain and suffering, past and future economic loss and past and future medical expenses. His adjusted life expectancy as a result of the injuries he sustained was taken into account when calculating future damages. In this case, the value of his future medical expenses was contested by the defense. We were able to overcome their arguments by retaining high quality medical and economic experts to compile a Life Care Plan that detailed the projected costs of medical care over his lifetime. By using irrefutable data, the Life Care Plan analysis was a significant factor in proving that at least 8 million dollars was going to be needed to fund his medical care over his lifetime. It is important to note that his wife had a claim for loss of services and consortium as well. In this case, the loss of services claim included compensation for the loss of having her husband's contributions to the home (e.g., home repairs and maintenance, lawn care, food shopping, household chores, childcare), as well as the loss of consortium (i.e., loss of a personal and intimate physical relationship, loss of quality of marital relations) both past and future. We were able to secure a 15 million dollar settlement for the family through meticulous preparation and attention to every element of our clients' damages.

Section 2: Wrongful Death

CHAPTER 4

WRONGFUL DEATH IN NEW YORK: THE BASICS

Wrongful death occurs when someone is killed as the result of someone else's negligence. An action to recover damages for a wrongful death can be brought as a result of an act of general negligence (e.g., automobile collision, work-related injury, premises liability) or medical malpractice.

New York's current wrongful death statute was enacted in 1847 and has not been updated to reflect societal and cultural changes of the past century. The law allows a grieving family suffering the loss of a loved one to recover only for the lost income from a family member who died due to a wrongdoer's negligence, but not for their pain and suffering. Simply put, surviving family members are not permitted to recover damages for their grief or loss. A surviving spouse is not entitled to their loss of the marital relationship. The only damages available to them are pecuniary (financial) loss and pain and suffering that the decedent experienced prior to death.

This law perversely places higher value on the lives of high wage earners, over those who earn little or nothing - such as children, stay-at home parents and senior citizens. Unlike the law in almost every other state, New York's antiquated law allows recovery only for pecuniary loss, which unjustly ignores the emotional damages of a wrongful death on the family, such as grief, loss of affection, and loss of counsel.

The New York State courts have frequently noted that our Wrongful Death Law is archaic and unconscionable. Time and again, courts have called upon the New York State Legislature to correct this historical anomaly – because recognizing only the financial cost, and not the human cost, of a wrongful death undermines the basic principles of justice that value and protect human life. Most notably, in Thurston v. State of New York, the court stated:

"Yes, hard cases make bad law, and the corollary is that bad laws make hard cases. The application of New York law to the facts of this case lead to the inevitable and very unpleasant conclusion that, although Defendant was negligent, and this negligence led directly to Cheryl Thurston's death, there can be no recovery in this action. I find cold comfort in the fact that I am not the only judge to have struggled with the fact that the laws of this great State appear to place no intrinsic value on human life. In Gary v Schwartz (72 Misc. 2d 332 [Sup Ct, Nassau County 1972]), the Hon. Daniel Albert eloquently lamented New York's "callous approach" to the valuation of a human life. He points out that our draconian wrongful death statute has changed little since 1846 (Lord Campbell's Act), when it grew out of exploitative child labor laws. "Since the appalling child-labor conditions have long since been eradicated, how can a formula based upon such a condition remain applicable?" (Gary at 338). The ultimate scandalous irony is that, had Cheryl been chattel rather than a human being, Claimant could recover the lost value of her property.

It is repugnant to the Court to have to enforce this law which places no intrinsic value on human life and is "no longer relevant and applicable to our contemporary social structure and mores" (Gary at 337). Although I add my voice to the chorus of those who would call upon our legislature to address this fundamental injustice in our wrongful death statute, I have no choice but to honor and faithfully apply the law as it now stands, and dismiss Claimant's action in its entirety."[1]

The injustice described so eloquently by the court has, like so many societal injustices, been

---

[1] Laurie A. Thurston v. The State of New York, 2013-031-019, NYLJ 1202602796553, at *1 (Ct. of Clms., NY, decided May 2, 2013).

deepened and exposed by the COVID-19 pandemic. New York's law prevents accountability for the tragic deaths of so many beloved grandparents and essential workers who put their lives on the line for each of us. The law acts as a shield for negligent actors, rather than protecting the most vulnerable among us.

Inequality in our civil justice system extends beyond the current crisis. One of the ongoing tragedies of our time is the horrifying incidence of maternal and infant mortality in our communities of color. Due to persistent discrimination, families of color are not only more likely to die in childbirth, they are more likely to be low-wage earners and less likely to be compensated for the unbearable loss of a parent or child.

New York's civil justice system is founded on the concept of holding wrongdoers accountable for the harm that they cause. The goal of this system is to compensate those who are harmed by others' wrongful acts and to deter negligent, reckless, and unlawful conduct. These sound principles can be best advanced by holding a wrongdoer liable for the full extent of the harm done, especially when the wrongful conduct causes the loss of a human life.

Wrongful Death Actions

Wrongful death actions in New York are governed by The New York Estates, Powers and Trust Laws (EPTL). EPTL, Section 5-4.1 which gives the right to the legal representative of the estate to bring an action for wrongful death. The right to recover damages for wrongful death is governed by EPTL, Section 5-4.3, and is known as a pecuniary (financial) loss statute. This requires the legal representative of the decedent to prove pecuniary loss which includes loss of support for the decedent's next of kin as a result of the loss of the decedent's earnings. In the case of the death of a parent who leaves surviving a spouse and dependent children, a claim may be made for any economic loss suffered by them. It is important to note that economic loss is not limited to loss of earnings. Loss of services to the decedent's spouse as well as loss of parental care and guidance to the decedent's children may be claimed, as can lost prospect of inheritance, medical and funeral expenses. In the case of the death of a child, loss of services to the parents may be claimed if there is evidence to support such a claim. Also of note is that a damage award will include interest from the decedent's death.

When an adult wage earner with dependents dies, the central components of recovery are loss of income and loss of parental guidance.

Plaintiffs utilize the expert testimony of economists to establish the value the decedent had to his or her family. Until recently, this testimony was not admissible when a stay-at-home parent died. Now, when the decedent was not employed outside the home, the financial impact on the survivors will not involve a loss of income, but increased expenditures to continue the services he or she was providing or would have provided if he or she had lived. Experts can help the jury evaluate the value of a stay-at-home parent's services.

Important for Clients to know:

Any settlement of a wrongful death case will need to get court approval. If the decedent left a will (which gets probated by the surrogate court), the items to be distributed out of the estate are set forth in the will. If the decedent dies intestate (without a will), there are set rules for how the court determines how the proceeds of a settlement or jury award are allocated and distributed in a wrongful death case. Furthermore, the court will scrutinize the terms, amount and circumstances of the settlement before approving distribution.

There are also different income tax considerations for medical malpractice and wrongful death cases. Just another reason why you must have an experienced attorney representing you in these matters. For example, in New York, in a medical malpractice/wrongful death case, juries are required to adjust damages downward for income taxes that decedent would have paid if he earned the income. However, in medical malpractice cases where the client is still alive, there is a downward adjustment, but it is done by the judge, not the jury. In non-medical malpractice wrongful death cases (personal injury/general negligence), taxes are ignored. Here, economic experts are not permitted to testify to the effect of taxes in non-medical malpractice personal injury cases.

Beware: there may be tax consequences if decedent owed back taxes.

CHAPTER 5

SEPARATE AND DISTINCT CAUSES OF ACTION

There are two separate and distinct causes of action for a death that occurs due to negligence in New York: survivorship and wrongful death.

The survivorship cause of action belongs to the deceased estate for the pain and suffering prior to death, whereas the wrongful death cause of action belongs to certain distributes, or survivors of the decedent who have suffered pecuniary (i.e., monetary) loss by reason of death.

For example, if a married parent was killed by a negligent driver who ran a stop sign, and the deceased experienced conscious pain and suffering before they passed, then the survivors (i.e., the spouse and children) would be entitled to compensation for the pain and suffering the decedent experienced prior to their death.

The wrongful death cause of action would entitle them to recover monetary losses that they sustained as a result of the death, assuming the deceased financially supported the spouse and children, and they did actually sustain financial loss as a result of the death.

When handling a wrongful death case, it is crucial that the attorney see the case as two separate and distinct causes of action, as each must be evaluated independently.

Survivorship Cause of Action

In order to bring a successful survivorship, claim for pre-death pain and suffering, there must be evidence that the decedent experienced cognitive awareness of pain and suffering prior to death. To accomplish this, it is necessary to investigate whether the deceased was killed instantly or experienced some period of pain and suffering.

One way to determine this is by interviewing the emergency medical technicians and those who were first on the scene. You must determine whether the deceased was still alive and had some level of consciousness immediately after the incident. It is crucial to determine whether the deceased showed signs of conscious pain and suffering (e.g., moaning, groaning, physical grimaces, complaints, yelling). Needless to say, it can be very difficult to find this sort of evidence and it requires due diligence on the part of the attorney and his or her team.

Once evidence of pre-death conscious pain and suffering is identified, the amount of time that it lasted also needs to be determined. Did it last five seconds, or an hour? Witness statements and medical records can aid in determining the answer. Based on the nature of the injuries, medical records, witness statements, findings on autopsy (pathology reports/slides are often helpful) an expert medical witness can provide a medical opinion as to the nature and length of the conscious pain and suffering experienced by the deceased.

The courts in New York have recognized "pre-impact terror" as an element of conscious pain and suffering. For this reason, it is important to look for evidence of the decedent having been aware of their impending death. An example comes from a recent New York case wherein a motorcyclist's use of the brakes provided evidence of pre-impact terror: the skid marks left on the road indicated that the motorcyclist saw the defendant's truck and was aware of the impending fatal collision.

Wrongful Death Cause of Action

The damages in a wrongful death claim are limited to fair and just compensation for pecuniary injuries. Such damages include loss of support, voluntary assistance, inheritance, medical expenses, funeral expenses, lost wages, and actual expenses. Pecuniary losses may include services such as cooking, cleaning, and driving family members.

Loss of consortium (i.e., the loss of a personal and intimate physical relationship between spouses) is not recoverable under the wrongful death statute; it is recoverable only under the survivorship cause of action, which covers the period of pre-death pain and suffering.

To illustrate this difference between wrongful death and survivorship causes of action, consider the following example:

The husband of a former client of Oddo & Babat, sustained a perforated bowel during an elective surgery, resulting in a massive infection and eventual death. He received weeks of treatment in the hospital before he ultimately passed away from his injuries. His wife was entitled to loss of consortium for those weeks he was in the hospital, but once he passed away, she was no longer entitled to any future loss of consortium, as post-death damages fall under the umbrella of wrongful death, which does not include loss of consortium as a recoverable item of damages.

The Statute of Limitations

The statute of limitations in a death case will depend on the cause of action. The statute of limitations for the survivorship cause of action is three years from the date of the accident or one year after the decedent passed away, whichever is longer.

The wrongful death cause of action carries a statute of limitations of two years from the date of death. However, there are exceptions to this rule, such as in the case of the existence of a related criminal matter. For example, if a drunk driver runs a red light and kills a pedestrian as a result, then criminal charges would be brought against the driver, and the decedent's personal representative would have at least one year from the termination of the criminal proceeding to file a wrongful death claim. This is true regardless of whether the two-year statute of limitations has already expired.

If the only surviving distributee is a minor, then the statute of limitations period is tolled until a guardian is appointed, or until that distributee has reached the age of majority, whichever occurs first. Again, as every case is different, it is imperative that you retain an experienced attorney who is familiar with these time limitations, as early as possible to protect your claim.

Chapter 6

The Wrongful Death Case Process

One of the first steps in the handling of a potential wrongful death case in New York is to confirm that there has been a death caused by wrongful conduct. There must be survival by distributees who have suffered pecuniary loss, which means that if none of the decedent's survivors relied on them for financial support in some way, then there would be no viable wrongful death claim. The pain and suffering damages, funeral and burial costs, and medical expenses speak for themselves; but it is obtaining the proof of loss of earnings and loss of financial support that is necessary and requires a lot of work.

Identifying the Defendant(s)

Identifying the defendant(s) in a wrongful death case depends on the facts and nature of the case. For instance, the defendant could be the driver and/or vehicle owner who caused a fatal automobile crash, or a property owner who fails to maintain his property in a safe and reasonable manner, or a general contractor who failed to provide the required safety equipment causing a fatal work-related incident. In a medical negligence case, any and all of the responsible parties can be sued. Had the injured party not passed away, whomever they could have sued for malpractice can be held liable.

Finding Evidence of Damages

Under the statute that dictates wrongful death recovery, the award of damages to the distributees of the decedent's estate is limited to the fair and just compensation for pecuniary injuries resulting from the deceased's death. Proving the right to compensation in this regard requires evidence of loss of support, voluntary assistance, possible inheritance, the cost of medical care, and funeral expenses.

If the deceased was a minor, bringing a wrongful death claim would require evidence of pecuniary or monetary loss to that minor's parents, which can be difficult to find. However, some situations involving a deceased minor do warrant wrongful death recovery. For example, in a wrongful death case involving a 16-year-old, my firm was able to show that prior to his death, the 16-year-old had been working part-time to help support his family; the deceased was from a first-generation immigrant family wherein all the members contributed to the financial needs of the household, so there was a monetary component to the claim.

To Litigate, or Not to Litigate

Deciding whether to go to trial or accept a settlement offer can be an extremely challenging part of the wrongful death case process, and involves many considerations. Sometimes a defendant will refuse to make a reasonable settlement offer. In that case, the client is left with no choice but to have a jury decide their case.

In general, trial is the last resort; clients have to understand that jury deliberations are not an exact science, and juries sometimes arrive at even the most unexpected conclusions. For this reason, heading to trial can mean heading into the great unknown. Many cases settle because few people want to take on that risk. That being said, your chances of success at trial will ultimately hinge upon your attorney's preparation and experience. I am a firm believer that there is no substitute for preparation. Even the most skilled courtroom lawyer will lose his case without meticulous preparation. He or she must not only be familiar with all aspects of the case, but also of the venue where the case will be heard, i.e., the potential make-up of the jury pool, experience in the community and knowledge of community feelings about the type of case you will be presenting. They should be familiar with the judges and well versed in the particular courthouse rules and customs. Make sure you find out how many cases the lawyer has tried in that venue. Retaining a highly skilled, experienced attorney is no guarantee of success, but it will certainly put you in the best possible position to succeed at trial or achieve an excellent settlement.

Should a client decide to pursue a trial and jury verdict, they must be thoroughly prepared to testify and fully informed and aware of all of the evidence and arguments on both sides. Preparing for trial is in itself a process that helps put the client in a better position to settle the case. The defense attorney will see that the client is willing to go to trial and the attorney is prepared and capable of presenting a strong case at trial, which often compels defense counsel to offer a fair settlement.

Factors for Consideration

One of the main factors to consider when deciding whether to take a case to trial is the strength of the evidence that has been obtained via the discovery process including the sworn deposition testimony of all parties. An honest and proper evaluation of the strengths and weaknesses of the case must be made at all stages of the litigation.

The second factor is whether an offer to settle has been made. The attorney is under an obligation to inform the client of any offer of settlement made by the defendant. This must prompt a thorough discussion between attorney and client about the "risk and reward" of rejecting the offer and proceeding to trial. If the defendant fails to make an offer, or makes a "lowball" or extremely unreasonable offer under the circumstances, the client may have no choice but to go to trial. However, if a fair and reasonable offer is obtained before trial, the client will avoid the risk, time, expense and stress that comes along with a jury trial.

That being said, the choice between a settlement or jury verdict is ultimately the clients to make; it is the attorney's job to provide a recommendation based on the facts, the evidence and in his or her experience, what is ultimately in the best interest of the client. The attorney must take the time to ensure that the client understands the reasons for that recommendation.

Discussions about a settlement versus a verdict at trial should happen throughout the course of a case, but even more so toward the end of a case when all of the evidence has been gathered and evaluated. Essential to this decision-making process between attorney and client is trust; the client must be able to trust their attorney's advice and recommendations. On the other hand, the attorney must be able to trust that the client is and has been truthful and will be cooperative in the preparation of the case.

Preparing for Trial: What Clients Should Expect

It is important for attorneys to give their clients an idea of what to expect during the pre-trial and trial phase of a wrongful death case. Make no mistake-the trial is no place for surprises, for both the client and attorney.

- ### *A Telling of Their Story*

During the course of the case, clients should expect to provide sworn testimony at a deposition (also called an Examination Before Trial or EBT). The client or witness will be asked questions under oath about the occurrence and the specifics of the damages claimed. This takes place outside of court, usually in the lawyer's conference room. During the deposition, the client will be asked questions by opposing counsel, the answers to which will be recorded by a court reporter. The questions will pertain to the relationship they had with the decedent, and the damages they have sustained as a result of his or her death.

Most clients are not only willing to provide this testimony, but eager to do so, because it gives them a chance to tell their story to the defense lawyer—the story about the person the deceased was, the value they added to their life, and what they have endured since their death. During the deposition process clients essentially relive the experience, which can be emotionally difficult, but it is also an opportunity to relay the weight of their loss.

Whether it is a client who was injured in a negligence or malpractice case, family members, or the personal representative of the deceased in a wrongful death case, giving sworn deposition testimony will most likely be necessary.

- ***Frequent Attorney-Client Communication***

Throughout the trial preparation phase—and especially during the exchange of discovery with the defendant—clients should expect to be in frequent contact with their attorney, and kept abreast of the case status at all times. They should also expect to meet with their attorney several times in order to prepare for the giving of testimony at a deposition or if necessary, in front of a jury (this can be a challenge for some clients, while others view it as a welcome opportunity to tell the jury about their loss).

Depending on the type and venue where the case is pending, it can take years from the initial filing to the time of settlement or trial, so the attorney needs to be made aware of any changes that have occurred in the client's medical condition, family dynamics or employment situation.

The client should expect frequent contact with their attorney and they should feel comfortable reaching out to the attorney at any time to discuss the status and progress of their case.

CHAPTER 7

THE VALUE OF A LIFE LOST

At the initial client intake interview, a lawyer handling a wrongful death case has the important job of explaining the law to their clients, as well as breaking down the practical considerations of bringing the case. Unfortunately, as detailed in Chapter 4, this often includes informing family members of a very difficult truth: they may not be entitled to compensation for the immense grief and sorrow they are suffering that was brought on by the loss of their loved one—whether it's a child, grandparent, or anyone else whom they were not financially dependent upon.

Understandably, this is a reality that for many clients feels impossible to grasp. How could their loss not be compensable? How could their loved one's life be said to have no monetary value?

At the outset, the attorney needs to explain how New York law applies to their loved one's case, and ensure that the client's expectations are in line with the reality of the law. This is much easier said than done, especially given the antiquated and nonsensical laws in New York which impact many of these cases (again, see Chapter 4).

It is equally important for clients to understand how important their role is in obtaining proof of economic damages (e.g., financial documents, witnesses, job habits or history, etc.). Often, clients possess information that their attorney cannot obtain from the records, so providing that information to the attorney can be very useful. Anything that the client believes might substantiate the claim of damages in the case should be provided to the attorney.

The Role of a Jury in the Wrongful Death Case

At trial, when it comes to the survivorship cause of action, the value is determined solely by the members of a jury, and is based on evidence detailing the decedent's experience immediately prior to death.

Not too long ago, Oddo & Babat, handled a wrongful death case involving a motor vehicle collision where our client died following extensive chest trauma. The autopsy showed that the trauma caused the decedent's lungs to fill with fluid, resulting in a slow, suffocating death. The jury concluded that the deceased was indeed consciously aware of pain and suffering prior to death, and found the manner of the death to be an extremely significant factor in determining what would fair and adequate compensation in the case.

If a jury returns a substantial verdict in favor of the plaintiff, the defendant may appeal the verdict if they feel that the verdict is excessive. The appeals court would then decide what a fair damages verdict should be based on the evidence in the case. Based on previous rulings by the appellate courts regarding the value of particular injuries, an experienced and well researched wrongful death attorney will have an educated idea of how the courts will handle a particular case on appeal.

When determining fair and just compensation for economic damages in wrongful death cases, the jury considers a number of factors, such as the age, health, and life expectancy of the decedent at the time of the negligence or at the time of the death. Their work life expectancy is calculated by an economist to determine how much the decedent would have earned over the course of their life. The jury can also consider the decedent's work history, work habits, future earning capacity, and potential for career advancement.

Proving Economic Damages

For the wrongful death action, the decedent's survivors are entitled only to compensation for pecuniary (economic) losses. The elements of wrongful death are (1) the death was caused by the wrongful conduct of the defendant; (2) that if the party had not died, they would have had a right to bring a lawsuit; and (3) the deceased's distributees suffered pecuniary loss by reason of the death. Obviously, the decedent cannot bring an action themselves, and there is no legal right for them to bring an action. Under the law, they need a personal representative to bring the lawsuit on their behalf.

If the deceased was the breadwinner of the family and in the prime of their work life, then proving economic damages would be relatively straightforward, assuming the help of economic, vocational, and/or occupational experts. In such cases, it is important to consider opportunities for promotions and advancement, fringe benefits, health insurance plans, and pension plans that would have been earned by the deceased.

It is important to know that economic experts do not merely crunch the numbers; they rely on medical reports, tax returns, and deposition testimony from employers and co-workers in order to render an opinion. Witnesses who can speak to the work habits and talents of the deceased provide useful evidence that an economist needs in order to render an accurate analysis and rock-solid opinion at trial.

CHAPTER 8

CONCLUSION: THE ROLE AND IMPORTANCE OF THE ATTORNEY

Clients hire wrongful death and medical malpractice attorneys during the extremely difficult and emotionally challenging times that follow tragic and catastrophic events. For the attorney, it follows that it is a very demanding line of work, both physically and emotionally that requires the attorney to share in the client's grief and loss. The attorney should be prepared to give those clients the attention and support they require and deserve.

Crucial to the attorney-client relationship during such trying times is the element of trust, and this means interacting with clients on a personal level, as well having empathy and an understanding of what they are going through—especially in the immediate aftermath of the death of a loved one.

There are always emotional and economic ramifications that flow from these catastrophic events, and there is never a clear end in sight. Even for those who survive life-threatening injuries, the impacts persist, whether through medical complications over the course of many years, additional hospitalization, years of physical therapy, or the numerous ups and downs that go along with these injuries.

These injuries do not just affect the injured; they affect everyone who is close to them. As a result, the attorney who handles these cases must become familiar with everyone who is involved, and remain prepared for the gamut of emotions. The attorney shares the lows with their clients, but they also get to share the highs, like learning that a once tragicallyinjured child has overcome great obstacles, graduated from college, or got married, had children, and lives a productive and happy life.

A wrongful death and catastrophic injury attorney experiences long-lasting relationships with their clients (many of mine have lasted for three decades!). On a number of occasions, I have represented different generations of clients from the same family, and I can say that I truly cherish those relationships. Making a positive impact on the lives of others is the most rewarding aspect of this profession.

Finding the Right Attorney

One of the most important things to consider when hiring a wrongful death or medical malpractice attorney is their level of experience. If an attorney only occasionally handles medical malpractice or wrongful death cases, then they likely are not the best choice; the chosen attorney should primarily concentrate on these areas of law, because as you can see from the previous chapters, they present unique and complicated issues.

On a professional level, the chosen attorney should be involved with trial bar associations and medical malpractice committees, and attend continuing legal education courses to stay current and sharp on all issues related to these areas of the law. Even better if they are the lecturers at those courses.

Truly understanding the complexities of the law is crucial. All too often, personal injury attorneys believe that they are qualified to take on medical malpractice and wrongful death cases. If they do, some soon realize that they are in way over their head. Over the years, I have received countless calls from those attorneys asking me for advice or asking if I can take a case over from them. Unfortunately, sometimes by the time they call, some level of damage to the case has already occurred. For instance, the attorney may have incorrectly identified the statute of limitations that applies to the case, and I may end up with a limited amount of time to investigate and start a lawsuit. Alternatively, the attorney may have missed critical pieces of evidence that are no longer retrievable or have been destroyed, or they misjudged the level of personal attention that the client needed.

Even if a lawyer understands the basic legal requirements to bring a successful wrongful death or medical malpractice case, it does not mean that they are capable of, or skilled enough, to provide the necessary follow-through to trial. These areas of law contain minefields, and the unsuspecting attorney who does not regularly practice in this area is liable to jeopardize their client's case. However, if you find an attorney who possesses the experience, skills, and knowledge of what it takes to successfully litigate these difficult cases, you will put yourself in the best possible position to win your case.

INDEX

Notes

Made in the USA
Monee, IL
05 November 2026

67387954R00048